Riding the Waves

Written by Mary-Anne Creasy

Flying Start
to Literacy®

Contents

Introduction

Surfing is an activity that almost anyone can learn to do. Riding the waves is exciting and exhilarating. But it's hard work and it takes a lot of skill to use the powerful force of the ocean for a great ride on a wave.

Surfing can be dangerous. When a surfer gets dumped by a wave, the force of the water pushes the surfer down under the water, and it is difficult to swim to the surface. Even professional surfers can end up killed or seriously injured by bad judgement or bad luck.

Having the right knowledge and experience helps surfers to survive.

Chapter 1

Wave riders

For most people, surfing is a hobby, but for some people it is a much bigger part of their lives.

Professional surfers

Some surfers are so good at surfing that they travel the world to compete in surfing competitions. They are professional surfers.

In a competition, surfers are judged on speed, control and the stunts or moves they perform while surfing. Judges score them according to the difficulty of the surfing moves and how well they perform the moves. The surfer with the highest score wins the competition.

Cutback – the surfer turns in towards the wave

Floater – the surfer rides the top of the wave
as it breaks

Tube-riding – the surfer rides inside the length
of the wave's tube

Aerial – the surfer becomes airborne off the wave

Extreme surfing

There are many places to surf that have huge, dangerous waves. The people who surf these waves have turned surfing into an extreme sport. These waves are so huge and sometimes so far from the beach that surfers have to be towed to them by jet-skis. Sometimes they are even dropped near the waves by a helicopter.

These surfers have travelled by helicopter to these huge waves that are far out at sea.

Extreme surfing on an enormous wave

This allows surfers to ride the biggest waves in the world. Sometimes they are over nine metres high. If a wave this size breaks on top of a surfer, the surfer can be pushed down nearly nine metres into the water. In the churning water far below the surface, the surfer sometimes cannot tell which way is up. It's important for the surfer to get to the surface quickly before the next wave hits.

Chapter 2

The world's best waves

The best surf is found on beaches that border large oceans.

Some of the best surfing beaches are in Australia, Hawaii, California and South America. These places have spectacular beaches that are well-known surfing hot spots.

Surfing on Oahu island in Hawaii

Hawaii

One of the best places to surf is Hawaii, a ridge of islands in the North Pacific Ocean. The islands are actually volcanic mountains rising up from a deep ocean floor. Shallow reefs close to the shore make huge waves for experienced surfers, while gentle waves in sheltered bays are perfect for beginners.

Pipeline

One of the world's most famous surf breaks, Pipeline, is on the Hawaiian island of Oahu. It is called Pipeline because powerful pipe-shaped waves are created by the shallow water and the coral reef. The pipe gets bigger and bigger until it is a giant, powerful tube.

A surfer rides Pipeline.

This surf break is so dangerous that some professional surfers have been seriously injured or killed while riding it. Despite this, a surfing competition is held there each year for the best professional surfers.

Chapter 3

Learning to surf

Almost anyone can learn to surf. This is Matilda. She has recently started surfing.

Q. **What skills and knowledge do you need to be able to surf?**

A. The most important thing is to be a good swimmer – this helps you feel comfortable in the water. Also, I think if you have good balance it is easier to stand up on the board and ride a wave.

Q. How did you prepare to learn to surf?

A. Spending time in the waves helps you know how strong they are and teaches you how to catch a wave. I spent a lot of time body-boarding before I began surfing.

Q. Did you ever practise surfing out of the water?

A. Yes, at home I practised getting up on a pretend board and doing things to help my balance, like bending my knees and putting my arms out. I also practised on a surfboard at the beach, before getting into the water.

1. Lie on your stomach. Pretend to paddle with both hands.

2. Put your hands down flat, next to your body.

3. Press up with both hands.

4. Lunge forward with one leg.

5. Bring your back leg to the front and turn to the side.

6. Keep your knees bent and raise your arms.

Q. What helped you when you began surfing?

A. When I first learned to surf, the instructor pulled me over the waves. So I just had to lie down, then she turned the board around and pushed me when a wave was breaking.

When I got my own board, my dad helped me by doing the same thing. Now I'm getting more confident.

Q. What would you tell other kids who want to start surfing?

A. Become a good swimmer and spend a lot of time in the surf, especially body-boarding, to help your confidence before you start surfing.

The water can be dangerous, and waves are stronger than they look, so only surf on small waves to begin with. I mainly surf in white water (waves that have already broken) because I don't feel comfortable with bigger waves yet.

Most importantly, practise a lot and be persistent!

Chapter 4

Staying safe

There are some basic rules that surfers need to follow. These rules help to keep people safe in the surf.

Keep fit and stay together

Surfers need to make sure that they are fit enough to go surfing, so that they can swim back to the beach if they lose their surfboards. People should never surf alone. By surfing together, surfers can help each other if they get into a dangerous situation.

Pay attention

Surfers always need to check the beach and the surf conditions before going into the water. Patrolled beaches are the safest places to surf, and surfers should always stay close to a lifeguard tower.

Signs and different coloured flags are often used to show how safe it is in the water. Surfers should always pay attention to these.

Rip currents

When a lot of large waves crash onto the beach quickly, a current called a rip is formed to carry this water away from the shore and back out to sea.

This water looks calm, so often people don't realise that it's extremely dangerous. The deep, fast-moving current can carry even a strong swimmer away from the beach at incredible speed.

When caught in a rip current, good swimmers can look for where the waves are breaking – this indicates shallow water and a sandbar. Then they can swim alongside the beach, not towards the beach, until they reach the breaking waves. For those who are not good swimmers, raising an arm will signal to the lifeguards to come and help.

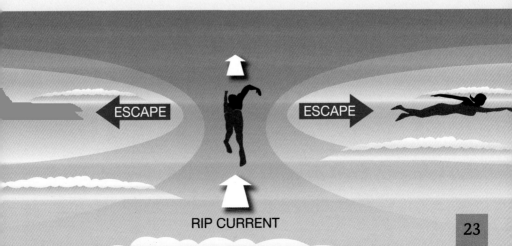

ESCAPE ESCAPE

RIP CURRENT

Protect yourself

Surfers should always wear sunscreen and a wetsuit or long-sleeved swim shirt. These help to protect them from the sun, wind and cold. Wetsuits also protect people from cuts and scratches and help them to float.

Falling off a surfboard is called "wiping out". The safest thing surfers can do if they know a wipe-out is coming is to jump into the water feet-first, covering the face. This helps to protect the face, head and neck from injury.

A surfer wipes out.

Watch out for others

A surfer needs to be aware of other people to avoid collisions. Surfers need to stay away from areas where people are swimming. A surfboard could easily hit a swimmer, especially if the surfer has fallen off.

Surfers should never surf on someone else's wave – they should wait for the next one. If a surfer tries to cut in front of another surfer, it's called "dropping in", and this is very dangerous.

A surfer drops in on another surfer's wave.

25

Conclusion

Many people love to surf and almost anyone can try it. Riding the waves brings a rush of excitement to all surfers, from beginners who are just learning to surf to professionals who make surfing their career.

Surfing is a lot of fun, but it can be very dangerous, too. It's important to be aware of the dangers, be prepared and stay safe.

Glossary

airborne

body-boarding

breaking wave

catch a wave

dropping in

rip current

surf break

tube

wipe-out

A note from the author

I loved researching this book. I became an expert in surfing history and terminology and I spent a long time on the Internet watching surfers riding the most enormous waves.

I live about an hour away from some great surf beaches, where my children learned to surf. My daughter went on a school camp where she had her first proper surfing lessons, so I asked her to show me how she was taught. We decided to put her experiences in the book to demonstrate the first steps of learning how to surf.